One day when we were —
I asked for a friend
of my own.
The very next day she
appeared.
And now she is sitting
here
beside me.
For Amy
With love,
Jean

Gratitude Journey

Ocean Shackleton

Love Matters Ministries
Burnsville, North Carolina

Published by:
Love Matters Ministries
86 Powderhorn Drive
Burnsville, North Carolina 28714

ISBN 978-0692601310

This book is dedicated to:

Virginia Lee Lintner,
Mother Extraordinaire;

my brother Herbert Shackleton,
real estate broker exceptional;

my sister, Ginnie,
phenomenal bank executive, mother of three
great young men and my lifelong best friend;

my little sister, Mary, now deceased,
who was always my staunch advocate;

my brother-in-law, Dick Parmelee,
stalwart supporter for much of my life;

and many others, too numerous to mention,
a complete list of whom would comprise an
entire book.

Acknowledgement

This book would not have come into being were it not for the encouragement and professional support of Pat Downing.

As transcriber, editor, graphic designer, and publisher, she transformed my pile of hand-written poems into this, my second volume of poetry.

With an eye for detail and her insistence on clarity, she gently pushed me to add the finishing touches that took some of my poems to the next level.

This process was truly an easy collaboration and enjoyable at every step.

Foreword

The poetry in this collection represents bits and pieces of a life-long accumulation. Beginning at an early age, Ocean observed his world and his own responses, and he preserved his impressions in poetry.

He has participated in many groups around the country, often winning the title of "Poet of the Month" with Poetry in the Woods in Ft. Lauderdale, Florida, and twice "Poet of the Year" with the East Coast Academy of Poets. He has also been published in numerous anthologies, magazines and newspapers.

For over 48 years, Ocean has been on a journey of inner transformation. Having participated many years ago in "Forum Training," offered by Landmark Education and the "Lifespring" program, he decided to re-enter that arena, "to knock the rust off."

Choosing to be a part of creating "peace in our time," he recently completed all the work in "The Gratitude Training," an intensive, three-part exercise in personal transformation.

The following collection of poems reflects that journey.

Patricia Downing

Contents

POEMS

SPECIAL BONUS
A TRUE TALE TOLD BY MY GRANDDAD

Particular

I am a particle of dust in an eternal wind
blowing me wherever it will, and yet I gather to
myself hundreds, perhaps thousands of particles
like myself, as I am borne on this conscious
breeze.

Together we form a universe, writhing in throes
of ecstasy and pain and gross indifference to the
wind that bears us whirling to a timeless destiny
shaped in each passing moment.

Breakthrough

So here we are, been here a while,
but we've been here before.
We'd go on to a better place,
if we could find the door.

The door to possibility
for a more fulfilling life.
A better life experience
with husband, friend or wife.

The place in which we find ourselves
leaves much more to explore,
plenty on our pantry shelves,
but still, we wanted more.

Our home is better than a hut,
work's somewhat satisfying.
Our friendships could be improved
there is no denying.

It feels like we are in a rut.
To achieve our dreams we're willing
to make a shift, to redesign,
find something more fulfilling.

Who said the grave is just a rut
with both its ends removed?
Feeling like we are enslaved
and can't escape the groove,

trapped, victims of circumstance,
doing the next right thing,
looking for a different dance,
wanting lives that sing,

We're dreaming of a melody,
a light and lively air
we'd be dancing to if we could see
the way to get us there.

We've met others from time to time
who had something so sublime
that we said "I want that too,
I'd like to make it mine."

It looks like their ship came in
while ours is in a wreck,
standing "at cause" within their lives
while we stand "at effect."

One day we button-holed some
whose lives were so appealing,
and heard of breakthrough training
whose potential left us reeling.

They said it's coming to our town
and we would have a chance
to embrace gratitude
and dance our special dance.

Communicating with the Infinite

I need only stop and ask
to experience the resurrection
of my purpose's reconnection.

I am infinitely linked
to the infinite. "I think
therefore I am." Twas said
by another long time dead.

But living evermore in me,
that perspective let's me see
that the creator and I are linked
by everything I'll ever think
and everything I'll ever do.
Observe, he's also part of you.

I'm aware there is no spot
I may go where God is not.

Time and Tide

The ebb and flow of life is sure
and like the sea is never ceasing.

And our forever search for more
always leads to the increasing
demands which life cannot fulfill
and leaves us racing, willy-nil
into a future still unknown
until we come into our own.

Perhaps we connect with a seer
who's found a way and shows it to us,
allowing Spirit ever nearer
until, like life, it pulses through us.

Listen for the voice of Spirit.
In the silence you may hear it.

Oxymoron

The blue moon rising silvery bright
illumined the hills below.
The silver cast upon the grass
caused them to look like snow.

Com trails crossed beside that moon,
reminding of the current strife,
the *war for peace* we carry on
at awful cost in life.

We demonize the "enemy"
and think they're ugly beings,
not noticing how they're so like us,
selecting what we're seeing.

Spring Things

Spring, and in this sunny room
we dispel the winter's gloom,
but there are those who never do,
their resentments peeping through.

Threadbare rags of their realities
seen in their elbows and the knees,
like fresh bathed dogs who throw a fit
and rush outdoors to roll in shit.

Each new beginning we have to thank
Creator that our canvas is blank,
our beliefs and actions the brush
that create depression or a rush
of joy and happiness and peace.

Choose the colors as you please.

Re-birth

.Ah, yes, now I remember
those dark nights of my soul,
with my insides torn asunder.
Would I ever be whole?

Would the sun that shone on others
shine again on me?
From the doom and gloom of my existence
would I once again be free?

I chose to forget myself
and help those who were lost.
In spite of all the pain I felt,
I didn't count the cost.

Now, spring has had its re-birth.
The flowers bloom once more.
Though one door has firmly shut,
I've found a different door.

Special Gifts

There are those who, well equipped,
give much. It seems to be their gift.
Well gifted with a bent for giving,
special people who make living
a joy that they pass on,
making it joyful to belong
to this, the holy human race.
They wear a smile on their face.

I had an experience today,
and my heartache went away.
I look forward to my giving
uplifting others, sweetening living.

Thank Creator for such sweet spirit.
It's Life's carol. One can hear it.

Random Acts of Kindness

Random acts of kindness prove
effective in learning how to love.
It's important not to mention
what we've done to gain attention.

This practice brings humility.
Its repetition sets us free.
Loving habit, as it's learned,
brings self-respect as its return.

Do good deeds and don't get caught
and see what living as we ought
brings us in the way of gifts,
and feel your spirit get a lift.

Dreams Come True

Dreams come true, but not by asking
while on the beach you're lying, basking.
They are not products of the sun,
but fruit born of the work you've done.

Work alone just doesn't do it.
You may work hard and come to rue it.
Though you seem to fail at all you try,
There is no cause for you to cry.

Dream your dreams and know them done
and keep on playing 'til you've won.
When you go the extra mile,
you will soon have cause to smile.

Our Word

Addressing the drift in order to shift,
we adopt "intention" to find new dimension.
Intention itself opens a door
to the dimension of our being more.

Much more is available than ever it seemed.
We're able to create all we have dreamed.
We implement intention with the power of
"word."
In its implementation each promise we heard
comes into existence in ways we can see.
It's in keeping our word that at last sets us free.

We learn to stand fast with what we speak
and in "being our word," comes the power we
seek.

Special

Like grains of sand upon life's beach,
not hugely different each to each.
Yet take away one single grain,
that beach shall never be the same.

There are perspectives we can take
about the differences we make,
but every single grain must matter
lest created by some "Mad Hatter."

Believe we each have a place
that's special to our human race.

Captain, My Captain

for Misha

The ebb and flow of time and tide
open vistas deep and wide.
That space into which I gaze
I cannot fail to be amazed
at this story, in no book
that is apparent when I look.

The story there on streets of gold
so delightfully unfolds
of the life that Misha lives.
She's radiant as she gives.

She gives herself in such a way,
lifeboat captain in her day,
an office where she earned her rank.
She has but herself to thank.

Val the Valiant

With vim and vigor
Val the victorious
re-enters life
in ways so glorious
as in competition
with the sun.
Now her new life
is begun.

For eons
it seemed a battle
and that is not
some useless prattle.

Now a new day
is begun
and she begins it,
Battle Won!

Richard's Grin

Grand plans for planetary change,
tribal commitment to rearrange,
brand new ways to transform matter,
tale now told by some Mad Hatter?

Or is it one that makes great sense,
a viable way of recompense
to repair the massive damage done?

When all the people become one,
upon that eventful day
when his wisdom shall hold sway,
the cards shall all fall into place
and bring a broad grin to his face.

Tatiana

She took a stand upon a chair
but almost no one saw her there.
She passionately bared her naked heart
and fervent wish to take a part
in the next step of Gratitude Training.
Caught up in their lives and time remaining,
her companions placed her on "ignore"
in their hurry to get out the door.

I saw her naked heart and cussed
then told the gathering that they must
pay attention to her passionate plea
and aid her in her quest to be.

They took a good look at themselves,
then reached into their pantry shelves,
giving freely of what they found
to help Tatiana stay around
and continue on her way.
She might be here with us today.
Unfortunately she is not.
Tatiana has been shot.

Tatiana chose not to go.
What she might have been,
we'll never know.
On the life boat she lost her space.
Now we'll never see her face.

I don't know what to believe;
I only know I grieve.

As it turns out I was misinformed.
A Tatiana indeed was killed,
but our Tatiana is unharmed.
Rejoice for she is with us still.

Marlboro Man

My little sister's crying.
It has broken her heart.
A mother and son
now torn apart.

Still a young man
with kids of his own,
with the Marlboro man
now he has gone.

Puff was no magic dragon
but an evil, toxic mist
that wrapped his lungs in an iron band
from the time of his first kiss.

In west Texas she held him
as he wasted away
writhing in the agony
of each passing day.

From Christmas through summer
till the cancer had won,
through infinite forevers,
devouring her son.

Her beautiful spirit
greatly diminished
from the time of its onset
'til its awful finish.

There's a heaviness inside
because my nephew Ricky died.
He fought cancer for a year
and now he is no longer here.

The Marlboro man took him away.
He puffed away and drank his beer.
Of side effects he had no fear,
and that is all I have to say.
I walked my path that very way.

Although I recognize the truth,
I did the same thing in my youth.
His penalty I did not pay
and I am still here today.

For every cause there is effect,
but I don't know what to expect.
How do I deserve God's grace
when we cannot see Ricky's face?

Jon's Gone

They said, "He's gone," but is that true?
He'll always be a part of you.
His gentle touch and ways of caring,
aren't those touches you are sharing?

No! It's not true! He's not gone.
Each of you shall pass him on.
He won't be gone until the day
all friends and family pass away.
Each of you shall pass him on.
It is not true. He is not gone.

Beyond the bend there is so much
that we cannot see or touch.
What some see as an ending
is but part of the trail's bending.

What some see as darkest night
is where the trail drops out of sight,
but just because we cannot see it
does not mean we shall not be it.

The Voice

Listen for the voice of Spirit.
In the silence we can hear it.
Spirit's voice is ever speaking
all the answers we are seeking.

Directions for making every choice
may be found in Spirit's voice.
In application love is found,
opportunities abound.

Why

Have you ever gone the whole day through
and not asked the reason why
you are, I am, or why the sun
moves slowly through the sky
or why it rains in Houston
while Miami's sky is clear
or why you wanted suddenly
to have a new friend near?

What power lies behind a thought
or rests within a deed
and why that tug from deep inside
to fill a human need?

What makes us tick, propels us on
when even hope is past
and at the end of our endeavor
gives sweet success at last?

In some form or another
I don't think I've gone one day
in which I didn't ask at least
one "Why?" or "In what way?"

There is a little child deep
within the heart of me
with an eternal restless
yearning to be
one with oceans in their churning
rush and swell to meet the land,
to pound upon the rocks of life
and reduce them all to sand.

I know this urge shall leave me
because it has begun to go.
I've found much of the "Why" of life
though there's more I wish to know.
I am begun to be at peace.
It feels so good to be
an ocean that's becalmed in love
and not the restless sea.

Chapel in the Garden

How do we remember
each life circumstance?
What part did we play
in this eternal dance?

Who was our dancing partner
as we whirled across the floor?
And what emotion did we attach
to remember ever more?

What person's ever present
within each story line?
The only face in the mirror
is forever mine.

"Father, Mother God," we ask,
"Unite us in our common task.
Fill us! Meet each human need
and let each loving act be seed
in universal gardens growing,
multiplying from each sowing.

As each loving act is done,
its warmth be greater than the sun
enveloping a fruitful earth
as love's new age shall have its birth."

The Unicorn

The unicorn is a mythical beast.
It really doesn't exit, you know.
So whenever you ride on a unicorn,
you may ride wherever a dream may go.

You can take off to Saturn,
detour to Mars
or ride off at a gallop
through the Milky Way's stars.

One red eye and one bright blue
make you believe they can see through you.
Beard of a goat and tail of a lion
that cracks like a whip when you take off flyin'.

Body of horse with legs of gazelle
lending it speed to run straight through Hell
without singing its coat, so pure and white
that wherever it goes, it lights the night.

Horn of unicorn tea will enrich your life,
cutting through trouble like a whetted knife.
I fell in love with a unicorn today
and the troubles I had just melted away.

When love of the unicorn fills me up,
laughter and joy overflow life's cup.
Enthusiasm always has its sway.
It collects negativity and blows it away.

Now those who would capture the unicorn
lurk in the forest in early morn.
A virgin with noose of white horse hair
by the side of the path stands, waiting there.

Woven by hands of fairies, they say,
with great incantations to keep evil away.
A spell of all spells in hair interwoven
to keep goblins and witches and spooks at bay.

A bunch of white grapes she holds in her hand
as she searches for unicorn tracks in the sand.
Then she hears his hoof beats coming
and she smiles at their drumming.

Sparkling dewdrop diamonds in the grass
like jewels, lie glistening as he prances past.
His nostrils flare as he sniffs the air,
entranced by the vision of the virgin fair.

Smiling, she extends her hand
that holds the bunch of grapes.
The unicorn starts nibbling,
the noose o'er him she drapes.

She laughs and hugs him playfully.
He kneels there in the sand.
She climbs upon his back and sits.
He rises on command.

Lightly, she grasps the horsehair reins
and whispers her desire.
The unicorn's feet move so fast
they set the trail on fire.

Just as the blazing comet's trail
winds and shows the way it goes,
the smoking, smoldering trail behind
the unicorn and virgin glows.

The unicorn is a mythical beast.
It really doesn't exist, you know.
So whenever you ride on a unicorn,
you may ride wherever a dream may go.

When Two Are One

Creating a vision and joining as one,
creating together more power than the sun,
explosive combination for ending confusion,
harnessing the power of nuclear fusion.

Swaying the will of the multitudes,
an expression of elation,
seeing the shining face of God
living life in excited creation.

We're each the sunshine
filling each other's day
and never shall Spirit
take sunshine away.

Little Things

Those little things you choose to do
have affected me for years.
Memories of kindnesses
have brought me close to tears.

Your face is always one I see
when I have thought of home.
Thoughts of you and others, too,
tell me I'm not alone.

I'm grateful for your presence
and hope you'll always be
near me like this and full of bliss
in close proximity.

The Masterpiece

It has begun, this brand new year.
We ask, "What is our purpose here?"
Finding the answer to that question
points us in the right direction.

Now, this may be very well for you
but what am I supposed to do?
Life's canvas is a total blank
and we each have ourselves to thank
for everything that's painted there.
So raise your brush and have a care.

With each and every stroke,
create a masterpiece, or joke.

Promises

Was there a promise that
an inner glow
would get so bright that
it would show
as light that beamed
from every pore,
ever brighter, always more
until the light should fill this room,
eradicating doom and gloom?

It has!

What one focuses upon grows.

Choice

Float out of here in the spirit,
leave our weighty mass behind,
approach Nirvana, as we near it,
adopt a Heavenly state of mind.

Dispel the context of scarcity,
notice plenty. Come and see.
In the land of great excess.
take notice that we are blessed.

On automatic, we're never free
until "at choice" has come to be.
There's no moment when we're not,
"choice" is all that we have got.

Step left and choose, step left again,
a step left waltz that we began
taking cover in the rain,
learning to step left again.

Transformed

In gratitude for Gratitude
I pen these loving words.
We experience transformation
because of all we've heard.

It's clearly not just the hearing,
but rests within the doing.
The hearing was the beginning
of our respective un-gluing.

We've taken off the masks we wore,
begun the process to restore
us each as our divine creation,
God's design, filled with elation.

Crystal ware filled to overflowing
with who we're being, where we're going.
We're going places collectively,
empowered, determined, wild and free.

Torch Tsunami

We pass the torch that some may live
because of how we stand.

Responsibility to carry on,
feed the flame now that they're gone
to celebrate what they've created,
that the flame for life is not abated.

We accept the torch today
and take our stand in such a way
that the crest of the wave shall swell,
encompassing every hill and dell.

Everyone shall have a chance
for Gratitude Training to enhance
the lives they said they would create.

We shall not let this wave abate.
A tsunami is what we make
to end all war and peace create.

Gratitude

Gratitude, like fine champagne,
is an effervescent drink.
The bubbles rise and fill us
just from what we think.

Spilling over from our hearts
in gifts to those around us,
seeking opportunities,
grateful they have found us.

Pops of possibilities
bursting in the air.
Lessons in loving
teaching us to care.

Caring for each other,
always an act.
Hearts overflowing,
giving it back.

SPECIAL BONUS

A TRUE TALE

TOLD TO ME BY MY GRANDFATHER

The Tale of the Whiffenpoof

Granddad was a fisherman. He learned to fish on his granddad's knee, as his dad had learned from his granddad. He came from a long line of fishermen, going back at least five generations. It was the family religion, passed on by the patriarchal side of the family.

He and his granddad had a favorite thicket of bamboo on the bank of the river. There they got the long, limber lengths of bamboo they used for fishing for bluegills, perch, croppy and bass. In the evening, they would set jug lines and trot lines to catch catfish and eels.

They made their own dough bait, which was the best in the area as measured by their catches. It was called Whiffenpoof Cheese because of its awful stench. Granddad said you had to have a good stench bait to catch catfish, and he sure succeeded at it.

His reputation as a fisherman and the maker of the Whiffenpoof Cheese led him and my dad to open their own tackle and bait shop in the little village in which they lived. They sold a lot of bait. Granddad's name was Harry West. West's Tackle and Bait was a huge success.

Harry didn't just use bamboo poles to fish. He acquired and sold all kinds of tackle. He loved to fool the fish and he created all kinds of bait and lures. He loved to whittle, and he made lures out of practically anything he came across, from beer can tabs to broken glass and metal scraps. He created creatures that wiggled and squirmed and glittered as they swam and dived through both salt and fresh water.

His lures caught fish, and that led to a partnership with his friend William (Bill) Spensor, who had a small factory that was capable of reproducing anything he made. Together they created a world of lures that caught both fish and fishermen. He made a lot of money in the process.

But the biggest part of Harry's popularity was his fishing skills. He had a reputation. He had caught the world's largest catfish. He caught it with his now famous Whiffenpoof Cheese and he caught it when he was only sixteen.

In those days, he lived with his mom and dad and the other twelve of his brothers and sisters in a rambling bungalow on the banks of the Mississippi in a very small village just upstream of the port. There was always a lot of activity with ships, boats, barges and even small craft of every description plying the waters constantly.

The river between his village and the port was treacherous. Often shrouded in fog, it was full of snags, shoals and a huge whirlpool called "the bottomless whirlpool," in which, it was rumored, lived the world's biggest catfish. Many were those throughout history who had tried to catch it. They would go out in the morning through the early morning fog and never be seen again.

The First Baptist Church had a memorial plaque on the wall in memory of those lost in pursuit of this goliath.

Harry used to listen to the stories of the old men who gathered around the pot-bellied stove at O'Leary's General Store on Main Street and drank coffee or whiskey, sometimes both, as was their habit, and told tales in a "Can you top this?" fashion.

They spoke, sometimes in whispers, with a sort of reverence about what they believed to be a behemoth catfish they all said was the world's biggest, that lived, according to legend, at the bottom of the bottomless whirlpool in the middle of the Mississippi about a mile downstream from where they lived.

The whirlpool, snags and shoals, which frequently shifted location, were on the river's navigation charts and were studied intently by the local river pilots who guided the ships through these treacherous waters.

Buoys marked the ever changing channels through which all of the river traffic ebbed and flowed. They had red and green lights and bells to aid in following them. The rule was "red, right, returning," which simply meant to keep the red buoys or lights on the starboard side of the ship when traveling upstream or away from the sea.

Many boats and ships had been lost before the installation of the buoys and channel markers. Harry listened raptly to these tales and began to plot to catch this catfish, in spite of all the legends that illustrated the adversities involved. He began to save the money he got from selling his catches of fish to the local restaurants as he planned and schemed to catch this mammoth.

He spoke to John Gallard, the local blacksmith, and together they designed the hook and leader to catch him. The hook was forged from two-inch tempered steel with twenty feet of logging chain as a leader to its six-foot length. The barb was basically the same as the harpoon in the movie "Moby Dick," sharpened to a razor's edge.

Harry went down to the port and purchased a length of two inch ship's hawser five hundred feet long. The coil of rope filled the entire buckboard.

With twelve offspring, Harry's mom needed an extremely long clothesline in their backyard to dry the volume of clothing in their twice weekly wash. It ran back and forth in a pattern that, from a distance, must have looked like a venetian blind. It was probably a mile long when it was all undone. Harry planned to use it to pull the barn door out into the current, with the coiled leader line and hook baited with his stench bait, when he finally made his bid to catch the fish.

After he had acquired all the above equipment, he began to create his bait. For a big fish, a big bait was required. Harry got a fifty gallon drum and cut one end out with a hammer and chisel. He rolled it down to the path along the river bank and began to collect every kind of dead animal he could find until the barrel was two-thirds full. He found rats, muskrats, weasels, birds, rabbits, squirrels and two skunks, which he put in the barrel.

Then he went down to the general store and bought four ten-pound bags of flour, one ten pound bag of corn meal and two pounds of sugar, and mixed them in a galvanized tub. When they were well mixed with river water, he covered his carrion collection with the mix, put fly screen over it all and left it for two weeks. It formed a big greasy stinking green lump.

On the day he planned to catch the catfish, Harry rose early, took off the barn door, drug it down to the water's edge and floated it out, tied to the mile of clothesline from his backyard. He then coiled the two-inch ship's hawser, attached to the logging chain with the hook on top, on the barn door. He rolled the drum to the door, dumped out the lump and impaled it on the hook.

With one end of the ship's hawser attached to the rear axle of the buckboard and the mules fed, watered and bathed with rose water to overcome the stench of the bait, he was ready.

Little Johnnie Patterson, age twelve, followed Harry around all the time. Harry was his idol. Harry allowed him to be part of the plan. Johnnie stayed with the mules and buckboard while Harry, shucked down to his shorts, tied one end of the clothesline around his waist and swam all the way across the river.

When he got to the other side, he had to rest a while. When he was rested, he pulled on the clothesline and pulled the barn door with the line, leader, hook and bait into the current to be carried into the whirlpool.

Harry dove in and swam furiously back to the shore and got to the buckboard just as the door got carried in the whirlpool and sucked into the depths.

As he mounted the buckboard it "commenced to jerking," as Granddad told it. He fought that fish all day and all night. Just as the sun broke over the horizon, the fish rose out of the depths and did a tail stand. It was so big it blotted out the sun, and when it fell, it caused a second dawning.

By this time Harry and the buckboard had reached almost to the top of the hill. The splash caused a tsunami so large that it washed away several of the tin shacks on the river bank.

Little Johnnie ran to the church and rang the bell to let everyone know that Harry had won the fight. The buckboard's rear wheels had been in the water three times during the tug of war that had taken place over night. Harry was exhausted when he drug that fish out across the mud flats and the townsfolk began to arrive with knives and buckets and tubs and pans to carve steaks from the fish.

Harold Baxter owned the town ice locker, a cave deep beneath the hill, where they kept the big blocks of ice they would cut from the lake each winter and sell all year for people's ice boxes. He brought three men with three buckboards, and along with the townsfolk, they carved catfish steaks from dawn until the moon shone on the fish skeleton.

Harold opened a chain of catfish restaurants throughout the south. Why, if you go down south today you may see them everywhere. Harry's services as a fishing guide were booked up two years in advance, and every year his popularity grew.

This is the tale as it was told to me many years ago by my grandfather, Harry West. There are many other tales he told me and as time passes, I shall relate them all to you.

Very truthfully yours,
Ocean Shackleton

.

Ocean Shackleton

Born June 8, 1938 to Herbert Skirving and Virginia Lee Shackleton in Abington, Pennsylvania, Ocean was the first of four children. He grew up writing poetry and he was a guest on children's programs.

Following a tumultuous childhood, Ocean enlisted in the United States Army as a 17-year-old, at the request of his mother, step-father and a judge. He served three years in Germany, developing an affinity for the language, and was discharged in New Jersey in April, 1959.

Ocean worked in manufacturing and landscaping, and he also made his living as an artist, a tree surgeon, bar tender, maitre d', waiter, cook, chef, house painter, journeyman carpenter, general contractor, alcoholism counselor and treatment center manager. Throughout his life, he continued to write poetry, committing to paper his observations of life and his thoughts and feelings.

During the 24 years he lived in the mountains of Western North Carolina, Ocean often shared his poems at local gatherings, and in 2017, he earned the silver medal for poetry in the Western North Carolina Senior Games.

He now lives in the beautiful mountain town, Burnsville, North Carolina, where he continues to write and share his poetry.

Want More of Ocean's Poetry?

If you enjoyed this book of poems, you may also appreciate Ocean's first volume, *Love Matters,* a collection of poems about all aspects of love - longing for love, experiencing the intimacy of love, and the aftermath of the loss of love.

To learn more, you may view the book on Amazon.

Made in the USA
Columbia, SC
09 September 2022

66287298R00035